797,88

are availab

Forgotten Books

www.ForgottenBooks.com

Forgotten Books' App
Available for mobile, tablet & eReader

ISBN 978-1-332-74804-4
PIBN 10432628

This book is a reproduction of an important historical work. Forgotten Books uses state-of-the-art technology to digitally reconstruct the work, preserving the original format whilst repairing imperfections present in the aged copy. In rare cases, an imperfection in the original, such as a blemish or missing page, may be replicated in our edition. We do, however, repair the vast majority of imperfections successfully; any imperfections that remain are intentionally left to preserve the state of such historical works.

Forgotten Books is a registered trademark of FB &c Ltd.
Copyright © 2017 FB &c Ltd.
FB &c Ltd, Dalton House, 60 Windsor Avenue, London, SW19 2RR.
Company number 08720141. Registered in England and Wales.

For support please visit www.forgottenbooks.com

1 MONTH OF FREE READING

at

www.ForgottenBooks.com

By purchasing this book you are eligible for one month membership to ForgottenBooks.com, giving you unlimited access to our entire collection of over 700,000 titles via our web site and mobile apps.

To claim your free month visit:

www.forgottenbooks.com/free432628

* Offer is valid for 45 days from date of purchase. Terms and conditions apply.

English
Français
Deutsche
Italiano
Español
Português

www.forgottenbooks.com

Mythology Photography **Fiction**
Fishing Christianity **Art** Cooking
Essays Buddhism Freemasonry
Medicine **Biology** Music **Ancient Egypt** Evolution Carpentry Physics
Dance Geology **Mathematics** Fitness
Shakespeare **Folklore** Yoga Marketing
Confidence Immortality Biographies
Poetry **Psychology** Witchcraft
Electronics Chemistry History **Law**
Accounting **Philosophy** Anthropology
Alchemy Drama Quantum Mechanics
Atheism Sexual Health **Ancient History**
Entrepreneurship Languages Sport
Paleontology Needlework Islam
Metaphysics Investment Archaeology
Parenting Statistics Criminology
Motivational

KANSAS HISTORY

BY

RAYMOND G. TAYLOR

INSTRUCTOR IN HISTORY AND CIVICS

KANSAS STATE AGRICULTURAL COLLEGE

1913

DEPARTMENT OF PRINTING
KANSAS STATE AGRICULTURAL COLLEGE
MANHATTAN, KANSAS

Copyright, 1913,
BY
RAYMOND G. TAYLOR

266220

A SYLLABUS OF KANSAS HISTORY.

INTRODUCTION.

This syllabus or outline of Kansas history is intended to serve a manifold purpose. Primarily it was the outgrowth of an attempt at a fairly thorough study of the territorial history of Kansas in its relation to national affairs, as a part of the course in United States history. For such use Sections IV and V of the outline will form the heart of the course, and Sections I-III will furnish the basis for a review of matters already treated in the course, while the sections on state history will serve for a like cursory review of important events succeeding the admission of Kansas to the Union. On the other hand, it is hoped that the entire outline may prove so complete and well balanced as to be of real service to teachers who desire to give a complete course in Kansas history.

Purposely the references have been limited to a list of books generally well known in Kansas and available to most of the schools of the state, either through school or public libraries, and to the collections of the Kansas Historical Society (cited as "Coll.") The exceptions are Kansas in The Sixties, a new book by Governor Crawford, and the Cyclopedia of Kansas History, published by the Standard Publishing Co., the third volume of which is devoted to biography. No reference has been made to works of fiction, yet the works of some Kansas authors, particularly the novels of William Allen White and Margaret Hill McCarter, should not be overlooked. Too much stress cannot be placed upon the importance of the Kansas Historical Society's Collections as an aid to teacher and student. Volume XII contains a very useful chronology or rather calendar of Kansas history. The list of county and local histories is by no means complete. It is intended merely as a suggestion.

While the outline is not based upon any particular book, for practical reasons the first reference in nearly every instance is to Prentis' History of Kansas, which is the state text and is in the hands of nearly every teacher and pupil in the Kansas common schools. This is in order that the outline may serve as a help in the common school course, first, and it is the hope of the author that this arrangement may give greater unity to the story of Kansas history and render this textbook more "teachable." Next follow references to Spring's "Kansas," Wilder's "Annals," and others, partly in order of their importance and partly of their availability in most Kansas communities, the exception being the "Collections," which are in nearly every case placed last for convenience. In many cases the textbooks in United States history will be of much importance in studying the national side of Kansas affairs. These are referred to merely as "textbooks." The larger works of Schouler, McMaster, etc., unless specifically cited, are referred to as "General Histories." In every case, unless otherwise stated in the outline, the references are to pages. These more extended references should serve for a high school, or even a short college course in Kansas history.

Finally, the author has tried to avoid the use of much controversial matter with which the literature of Kansas history is so plentifully deluged. To eliminate all material of that character is clearly impossible, for as yet much of the most valuable of our historical writing is the work of active participants in the stirring history of our early days and necessarily is personal.

Manhattan, Kansas, January 6, 1913. R. G. T.

A SYLLABUS OF KANSAS HISTORY.

I. Spanish and French Period. 1540-1803.

1. SPANISH EXPLORATION.
    a. Coronado, 1540-'41. Quivira. Harahey.
    b. Padilla, 1541.
    c. Onate, 1601.
    d. Villazur, 1720.

(a) Prentis, Ch. II; Spring, 17-19; *Annals*, 5-8; Andreas, 44-5; Winship, *Journey of Coronado;* Winsor II, Ch. VII; Bureau of Ethnology Reports, Vol. 14; Brower, "*Quivira*," "*Harahey;*" *Coll.*, VI: 125-7, 477-85; VII: 20-1, 40-6, 270, 364, 573; VIII: 141, 152-63 (map); X: 68-80 (map), 84-7, 529-30; XI: 582; XII: 219-52 (map), very good. (b) *Coll.*, X: 84-7, 472-9. (c) *Coll.*, X: 87-98. (d) *Coll.*, XI: 397-423.

2. FRENCH EXPLORATION.
    a. La Salle and the French in Louisiana.
    b. M. du Tissenet, 1719, and M. de Bourgimot, 1724.

(a) Textbooks; Winsor IV: Ch. V (esp.); Fiske, *Discovery* II, Ch. XII; Parkman, *La Salle and the Great West*. (b) Prentis, Ch. III; Spring, 19-20; *Annals*, 10-11; Andreas, 47-9; *Coll.*, IV: 276-80; IX: 250-7, 574-6; X: 336-8.

3. TREATY OF PARIS, 1763.

Textbooks; General Histories; Prentis, 28; text of treaty in Macdonald.

4. TREATY OF SAN ILDEFONSO, 1800.

Textbooks; General Histories; Macdonald, introductory note to treaty of 1803.

5. LOUISIANA PURCHASE, 1803.

Textbooks; General Histories; Prentis, 28-30; *Annals*, 15-18; text of treaty in Macdonald, *Treaties and Conventions* and U. S. *Statutes at Large*, Vol. 8. (Boundaries of Louisiana defined and limited by treaty with Spain, 1819. All of that portion of present

State of Kansas west of 100th meridian and south of Arkansas river belonged to Spain, the rest to U. S. Textbooks; text of treaty in *Annals*, 23, and other references as for treaty of 1803. Maps in Prentis, Textbooks, and Hart's *Epoch Maps*.)

II. Pre-Territorial Period: 1803-1854.

1. AMERICAN EXPLORERS IN KANSAS.
   - a. Lewis and Clark, 1804.
   - b. Pike, 1806-'07. Pawnee Republic.
   - c. Long, 1819.
   - d. Fremont, 1842-'48.

(a) Textbooks; Prentis, 31-2; *Annals*, 19-20; Andreas, 49-50; Original Journals of expedition; Wheeler, *Trail of Lewis and Clark*; *Coll.*, passim. See indexes, Vols. VII-XI. (b) Textbooks; Prentis, 32-40; *Annals*, 21; Andreas, 50-53; Pike's *Journal*; *Coll.*, VI: 325-36; VII: 261-317 (esp. 301-17); IX: 574 (and map); X: 15-119 passim, esp. 54-68. (c) Textbooks; Prentis, 40-1; *Annals*, 23; Andreas, 53-4; *Coll.*, IX: 574 (and map) and indexes Vols. VII-IX. (d) Textbooks; Biographies; Prentis, 41; *Annals*, 34; *Coll.*, IX: 559, 575-6 (and map).

2. THE DAYS OF THE TRAILS.
   - a. Santa Fé.
   - b. Oregon and California Trails.
   - c. Other Trails.

Prentis, Ch. V; Andreas, 54-7; Holloway, Ch. VIII; Inman's Works; *Echoes of Pawnee Rock; Coll.*, I and II: 270; V: 88-93, 93-99; VIII: 67-71, 137-43; IX: 552-78; XI: 456-63; XII: 253-60, 261-69.

3. TRADING POSTS.
   - a. Westport Landing.
   - b. Council Grove.
   - c. Mission Creek. Trading Post. Others.

Prentis, 64; *Annals*, 27, 30, 37, and passim; Holloway, Ch. VIII; *Coll.*, IX: 233, 565-78 (and map); XII: 426-90.

4. MISSIONS.
> *a.* Denominations.
> *b.* Locations. Mission Schools.

Prentis, Ch. VIII; *Annals*, passim; Andreas, 66-74; *Coll.*, I and II: 263-78; VIII: 250-71; IX: 152-230, 565-78 (and map); X: 312-25; XII: 65-9.

5. MILITARY POSTS.
> *a.* Leavenworth.
> *b.* Fort Scott.
> *c.* Fort Riley.

Prentis, 64; *Coll.*, I and II: 263-70; IX: 565-78 (and map).

6. THE INDIANS IN KANSAS.

Prentis, Chs. VI and VII; *Annals*, passim; Andreas, 58-65; Geary in Kansas, Ch. II; *Coll.*, I and II: 280-301; VIII: 72-109; 171-7, 206-12; IX: 73-88; X: 327-413; XI: 333-395; XII: 183-193.

7. POLITICAL HISTORY IN OUTLINE.
> *a.* Organization of Louisiana Territory, 1804.
> *b.* Louisiana Territory Renamed Missouri Territory, 1812.
> *c.* Indian Country, 1820. Missouri Territory Minus State of Missouri and Arkansas Territory.
> *d.* Indian Country Limited, 1830.
> *e.* Indian Country Named, 1834.
> *f.* Treaty of Guadalupe Hidalgo, 1848. Rest of What Is Now Kansas Brought Under Control of U. S.
> *g.* Compromise of 1850. Texan Cession to U. S. and Establishment of Squatter Sovereignty Doctrine in Utah and New Mexico.

(*a*) *Middle Period*, 55-6. (*b*) Babcock, *Rise of American Nationality*, 257; *Middle Period*, 56. (*c*) Map in Turner, *Rise of New West*, op. p. 114. (*d*) Prentis, Ch. VI. (*e*) *Annals*, 30. (*f*) Textbooks; text of treaty in Macdonald, *Source Book* and *Select Documents*, and in *Statutes at Large*, Vol. 8, and *Treaties and Conventions*. (*g*) Textbooks; General Histories; text of bills in *Statutes at Large*; Macdonald, *Select Doc.*, 378; *Source Book*, 383-394.

III. Slavery in the Territories. A Brief Review.

General References: Textbooks. General Histories.
1. Missouri Compromise.
2. Texan Rebellion and Annexation.
3. Mexican War.
4. Wilmot Proviso.
5. Compromise of 1850.
6. Growth of Squatter Sovereignty Idea.

IV. The Kansas-Nebraska Bill. 1854.

General References: Textbooks; Larned; Lalor; Rhodes, Vol. I, 439-500; Schouler, V: 279-93; Von Holst, (1850-'54) Chs. VI-VIII; *Middle Period*, Ch. 19; Ray, *Repeal of Missouri Compromise; Coll.*, IX: 115-126; Macdonald, *Source Book*, 403; *Sel. Doc.* 403; Prentis, 346-351.

1. HISTORY OF THE BILL.

Prentis, Ch. IX; Spring, 2-16; *Annals*, 40-5; Andreas, 81-2; Holloway, Ch. VI; *Geary in Kansas*, Ch. III; Textbooks; General Histories cited above; *Cong. Globe*.

2. BOUNDARIES, POPULATION, ETC.

Prentis, 71-2; *Annals*, 45-6; Andreas, 81-2; Hale, *Kanzas and Nebraska;* text of act; *Geary in Kansas*.

3. PRINCIPLE—SQUATTER SOVEREIGNTY.

Prentis; Spring; Textbooks; Biographies of Douglas and text of act.

4. RECEPTION IN DIFFERENT SECTIONS OF THE COUNTRY AND BY DIFFERENT GROUPS. Anti-Nebraska Democrats.

Textbooks; Prentis, 70; Rhodes, II: 58-74; Schouler, V: 293, 301, 307-308, 314; Ames, *State Documents on Federal Relations*, 280-288.

V. Kansas Territory. May 30, 1854, to January 29, 1861.

General References: Textbooks; Rhodes II, Chs. VII-IX; Schouler, V: 315-421; *Middle Period*, Chs. XX and XXII; Lalor; Larned; *Cyclopedia of Kansas History*, Vols. I and II; Prentis; Spring; *Annals;* Andreas; Smith, *Parties and Slavery*, Chs. VII-XI, XV-XVI; Hart's *Contemporaries*, IV, Ch. VI; *Coll.*, I and II: 115-42; III: 338-469; VI: 175-186, 336-42; IX: 120-142 (esp. good).

1. EMIGRANT AID. Planting of Kansas. Towns. Conflicts.
    a. Free State Efforts.
    b. Pro-Slave.

(a) Prentis, 73-6; Spring, 29-36, 38-40; *Annals*, 42, 43, 46-51, 58, 70, 153; Andreas, 83-6; Thayer, *Kansas Crusade;* Robinson, *Kansas Conflict*, Chs. II-IV; Mrs. Robinson, *Kansas, Its Interior and Exterior Life; Geary in Kansas*, Ch. IV; *Coll.*, I and II: 186-202; V: 30-41; VI: 90-96; VII: 322-61; VII: 467-70. (b) Prentis, Ch. X; Spring, 24-29, 41; Andreas, 83-6; *Annals*, passim; *Geary in Kansas*, Ch. IV; *Kansas Conflict; Am. Hist. Rev.*, 6: 38-48; Holloway, Ch. X.

2. ORGANIZATION OF THE GOVERNMENT, 1854-'55.
    a. Reeder, Governor.
    b. Elections. Nov. 29, '54, Mar. 30 and May 22, '55.
    c. Pawnee Legislature. "Bogus Statutes." Slave Code.
    d. Territorial Courts. Judge Lecompte.
    e. Reeder's Recall.
    f. Beginnings of Violence. Missouri Border.
    g. Territorial Journalism.

Prentis, Ch. XI; Spring, Ch. IV; *Kansas Conflict*, Chs. VI and VII; *Annals*, 57-75 and passim; Holloway, (a) Ch. XII, (b) Ch. XIII, (c) Ch. XV, (e) Ch. XVI; (c) *Statutes of Kansas Territory*, 1855, and appendix to "*Three Years on the Kansas Border.*" Andreas, 87-97, 101-5. (f) *Recollections of Pardee Butler*. (g) *Annals*, 165; *Coll.*, I and II: 145-56, 164-82; (a) III: 197-223 (Biog. Reeder). General References: *Coll.*, III: 223-278 and V: 163-234 (Documentary History of Administration); VI: 371-82; VII: 361-73; VIII: 227-50.

3. ADMINISTRATIONS OF SHANNON AND GEARY. Sept., '55, to Mar., '57. Topeka Movement and Civil War in Kansas.
    a. Big Springs Convention.
    b. Territorial Elections. Oct. 1-9, '55.

c. Topeka Convention.
　　d. The Topeka Constitution.
　　e. "Law and Order" Movement.
　　f. Further History of the Topeka Constitution and Government.
　　g. Congressional Investigating Committee.
　　h. Wakarusa War. Murders of Dow and Barber. Leaders of Freesoil Party—Robinson, Lane, Brown, et al.
　　i. Arrest and Trials of Free State Leaders.
　　j. Sack of Lawrence. May 21, 1856.
　　k. War in Eastern Kansas Counties. John Brown.
　　l. Reign of Violence, 1856-'57. Missouri Border.
　　m. Second Territorial Legislature.
　　n. Preparations for New Constitutional Convention.
　　o. Characters of Leaders—Robinson, Lane, Brown, Atchison, Stringfellow, and Others. Shannon and Geary.

Prentis, Chs. XII, XIII; Spring, Chs. V-IX; Holloway, Chs. XVII, XVIII, XX-XXIII, XXVIII, XXIX, XXXI; *Annals*, 75-158 passim, esp. 75-7, 85, 87, 90-106, 109, 120-2, 139, 142, 146, 147; Andreas, 111-2, 114, 116-122, 125-36, 155, 169, 299, 301; *Kansas Conflict*, Chs. VII-XIII; *Geary in Kansas; Six Months in Kansas;* good general references. (*o*) Biographies, Prentis, 133-36, 310-11; *Cyclopedia of Kansas History*, Vol. 3, Biographies of Lane by Speer and Connelly, Blackmar's Robinson, and Biographies of Brown by Sanborn, Connelly, Villard, Von Holst, Redpath, and Newton; Spring, *A Kansas Politician* [Lane], *Am. Hist. Rev.*, 4: 80-104, *Coll.*, (indexes). *Coll.*, IV: 373; V: 42-7; (*h*) V: 74-87; VI: 77-83; (*d*) VI: 292-305; VII: 521-536; (*k*) VIII: 177-87, 302-15; (*o*) VIII: 199-205, 275-89; XII: 338-46; (*a*) VIII: 362-77; (*f*) IX: 540-5; (*h*) X: 457-71.

4. WALKER AND DENVER. Mar., '57, to Oct., '58. Lecompton. Balance Turns in Favor of Free State Men.
　　a. Election of Delegates to Lecompton Convention.
　　b. Free State Convention at Grasshopper Falls.
　　c. Territorial Election. Oct. 5, 1857.
　　d. Lecompton Convention.
　　e. Lecompton Constitution.
　　f. Elections on the Constitution. Dec. 21, '57, Jan. 4, '58.
　　g. Free State Convention at Lawrence.
　　h. The Territorial (Free State) Legislature. Its Work. Its Troubles.

KANSAS TERRITORY 11

    i. The Topeka Legislature. End of the Topeka Movement.
    j. Lecompton Constitution in Congress. Candle Box Fraud. The English Bill.
    k. Final Election on the Constitution. Aug., '58·
    l. War in Southeastern Kansas. Marais des Cygnes Massacre.
    m. Enabling Act of 1858. Veto.
    n. Minneola and Leavenworth Conventions. Leavenworth Constitution.
    o. Election of May 18, 1858.
    p. Brown's Return and the Missouri Raid.

Prentis, Chs. XIV, XV; Spring, Chs. IX-XII; *Annals*, 155-242 passim, esp. (*a*) 155, 161, 165; (*b*) 176; (*e*) 177-191; (*g*) 199, 202-3; (*h*) 207-8; (*j*) 210, 231-3; (*k*) 238-40; (*l*) 236-7; (*n*) 215-30. Andreas, 162-9; Holloway, Ch. XLI; Brown, *Rescue of Kansas;* Ames, *State Doc.*, 299-303; (*e*) Macdonald, *Sel. Doc.*, 435-7; *Source Book*, 420-3; Rhodes, II: 278-301; Schouler, V: 382-99; *Middle Period*, 460-71; Tomlinson, *Kansas in 1858. Coll.*, (*n*) III: 5-15; (*l*) VI: 365-70; (*p*) VIII: 443-9; (*h*) X: 169-216; (*j*) X: 216-32; (*j*) A. H. A. Repts. I: 199-210 (1906).

5. GOVERNOR MEDARY, NOV., '58, to DEC., '60· Close of Territorial Period.
    a. Fourth Territorial Legislature.
    b. Enabling Act of Feb. 11, 1859.
    c. Wyandotte Convention.
    d. Wyandotte Constitution.
    e. Fifth Territorial Legislature.
    f. Election of Dec. 6, 1859.
    g. Wyandotte Constitution in Congress, Apr., '60, to Jan., '61·
    h. Summary: Constitutions of Kansas. Capitals of Kansas.

Prentis, Ch. XVI and pp. 136-9, 352-5, 356-82; Spring, 262-7; *Annals*, 248-78 passim, esp. 261-76, 310; Andreas, 172-6; Holloway, Ch. XLIX; Bates, *Civics of Kansas*, 67-80; Hodder, *Civil Government of Kansas;* John A. Martin, *Addresses*, 17-36; *Coll.*, (*c*) I: 236-47; (Gen. Ref. Hist. of Admin.) V: 561-633; (*c*) VII: 130-51, esp. good; (*h*) VIII: 331-51; (*d*) XI: 47-52, also *General Statutes of Kansas*, and *Constitution of Kansas* pub. by Crane & Co. for text of constitution and history of amendments; (*h*) XII: 331-7.

6. SOCIAL AND ECONOMIC DEVELOPMENTS IN KANSAS. 1854-'61.

  a. Population. Growth. Distribution.
  b. Pioneering in Kansas.
  c. Agricultural Conditions. Progress. Drouth of 1860.
  d. Towns and Trade. Highways. Steamboat Lines.
  e. Early Churches and Schools. Journalism.
  f. Slavery in Kansas.

Prentis, 72, 106-7, 114-5, 129-31; Spring, 319-24; *Annals*, passim; Andreas, passim; Holloway, Ch. XXIII; Cordley, *Pioneering in Kansas, History of Lawrence;* all county and local histories and annals; Tomlinson; Boynton and Mason; Brewerton; Mrs. Robinson; *Six Months in Kansas;* John A. Martin, *Addresses*, 7-14, 158-195, 202-5; *Kansas Annual Register* for 1864; *Coll.*, I: 203-18; (*f*) VII: 225-42 (good); VII: 441-6; (*c*) IX: 8-19; (*b*) IX: 126-143; (*e*) IX: 231-5; (*d*) IX: 317-58, 565-78 and map; (*b*) XI: 594-613; (*e*) XII: 135-82; (*b*) XII: 353-8; (*d*) XII: 426-56.

VI. Kansas in the Civil War. 1861-1865.

General References: Records of Rebellion; Crawford, *Kansas in the Sixties;* Blackmar, *Life of Robinson;* Speer, *Life of Lane; Kansas Annual Register* for 1864; *Annals*, 308-426 passim; General Histories; Prentis, Chs. XVII, XVIII; Spring, Ch. XIII; Martin, *Addresses; Cyclopedia of Kansas History; Collections.*

1. ROBINSON GOVERNOR. Organization of State Government.

Prentis, 141-3; Spring, Ch. XIII; Blackmar's *Life; Coll.*, VI: 87-202.

2. ACTION OF THE LEGISLATURE. U. S. Senators.

Prentis, passim. Secs. 162, 165, and 178. Spring, 272 282 and following. *Annals*, passim. Andreas. *Coll.*, X: 414-28.

3. KANSAS REGIMENTS AND SOLDIERS IN THE CIVIL WAR.

Prentis, Secs. 165-7, 169-70, 172-6, 179, 191-4, 196-9, 204-7; Spring; *Annals*, 328-41, 362-5, 368; John A. Martin, *Addresses*, 14-

16, 36-49, 217-22; *Am. Hist. Rev.*, 4: 80-104. *Coll.*, VIII: 271-75, 352-362; IX: 430-43, 455-60; XI: 217-53; XII: 271-95; V: 116-27.

4. GOVERNOR CARNEY.

See indexes of Historical Society Collections.

5. WAR ON KANSAS SOIL. Quantrill's Raid. Price's Raid.

Prentis, Secs. 168, 171, 180-9, 200-2; Spring; *Annals*, 370-2; Cordley, *History of Lawrence; Kansas Annual Register*, 1864, pp. 146-167 and following; *Coll.*, VI: 305-12, 317-25; VII: 161-7; VIII: 149-151; XII: 401-4.

6. BEGINNINGS OF THE STATE.
   - a. State Organization. State and National Politics in Kansas. Parties and Elections.
   - b. Economic and Social Growth. Railroads. Homestead Law. Growth in Population and Wealth. Social Conditions.
   - c. Boundary Lines of Kansas.

(a) Prentis, Secs. 177, 212; Spring, Ch. XIII, passim. *Annals. Am. Hist. Rev.* 4: 80-104; references for "1" and general references as above. (b) Prentis, Secs. 178, 208-211; Spring; *Annals*, 341; Jenkins, *Northern Tier;* Stark, *Annual Register* for 1864; *Coll.*, esp. XI: 80 and following and XII: 37-64. Census Reports; U. S. Statistical Abstracts. (c) *Coll.*, XI: 53-80; Proceedings Miss. Valley Hist. Assoc., III: 58-72.

VII. Kansas, 1865-1898. Period of Struggle and Attainment.

General References: Prentis, Chs. XIX-XXIX; Spring, Ch. XIV; *Annals* (good to 1885, date of pub.); Andreas, 209-43 (pub. 1883); John A. Martin, *Addresses*, 119-37.

1. GROWTH IN POPULATION. Organization of Counties. Growth of Towns. Immigration. Negro "Exodus."

Prentis, Secs. 215, 230, 232, 240-2, 261-2, 306-8, and appendix; Martin, *Addresses*, 158-65; *Coll.*, IV: 287-8; VII: 472-86; VIII: 449-72 (very good); IX: 485-97; X: 485-533; XI: 19-46; XI: 489-528; XII: 426-90.

2. INDIAN WARS, 1865-'69. Indian Lands. Reservations.

Prentis, Secs. 216-23, 228, 267, 291-2; Crawford, *Kansas in the Sixties; Coll.*, V: 69-71; VI: 35-52, 147-69, 344-57; VII: 47-83; VIII: 110-17, 187-99; IX: 66-72, 443-54; X: 7-14, 295-311, 428-56; XI: 529-49; XII: 1-10, 296-302.

3. HARD TIMES. Drouths. Grasshoppers.

Prentis, Secs. 243-5; Spring, Ch. 14; *Coll.*, indexes of all volumes.

4. BOOM PERIOD, 1880-'90. Causes. Characteristics. Results.

Prentis, Sec. 288; Spring, Ch. 14; *Coll.*, IX: 426; XI: 176-8; indexes to all volumes.

5. PERIOD OF DEPRESSION.

Prentis, Secs. 215, 231, 282, 300-4, 350, 356-7, 366-7; Spring, Ch. 14; *Coll.*, indexes to all volumes.

6. INDUSTRIAL DEVELOPMENT.
   - *a.* The Frontier.
   - *b.* Agriculture.
   - *c.* Railroads.
   - *d.* Mining.
   - *e.* Manufacture.

Prentis, Secs. 215, 229, 231, 232, 233, 282, 290, 300, 304, 313, 325, 326, 350, 357; Spring, pp. 308-12; *Coll.*, VII: 47-83, 84-95, 198-202, 243-60, 459-64; VIII: 143-8; IX: 33-44; XI:529-49; XII: 347-52, 383-7; Martin, *Addresses*, 119-37, 171-2.

7. POLITICAL HISTORY.
   - *a.* Parties and Elections. Governors. U. S. Senators and Representatives.
   - *b.* Legislative Advance.
   - *c.* Constitutional Amendments. Prohibitory Amendment.
   - *d.* The Populist Movement.
     1. Agricultural Depression.
     2. Alliance Movement. Other Similar Organizations.
     3. Formation of Populist Party. In State. In Nation. The Platform.
     4. Populist Reign in Kansas.

(*a*) Prentis, passim; *Coll.*, IX: 378-430; indexes of all volumes for Governors; (*b*) Prentis, Secs. 251, 287, 298, 299, 301, 323, 355,

364; *Coll.*, passim; (c) Prentis, Secs. 249, 252, 253, 258, 259, 260, 359. *Annals*, passim, esp. 931-3; Andreas, esp. 288-91; (d) Prentis, Secs. 234, 317-24, 334-42; *Coll.*, VII: 121-6; 453-8; VIII: 140; IX: 1-8; for topic d the periodical literature of the early "ninety's" is especially good. Look in indexes of current literature under catchwords "Alliance," "Farmers' Alliance," "Grange," "People's Party," "Populist Party," "Peffer," "Lease, Mrs.," etc.

VIII. The New Kansas. 1898-1913.

General References: Prentis, Chs. XXIX-XXXIV; Spring, Ch. 14; Becker, *Kansas*, in Turner, *Essays*, pp. 85-111; *Cyclopedia of Kansas History; Collections;* Periodical Literature; "Session Laws" of Kansas.

1. KANSAS IN THE SPANISH-AMERICAN AND PHILIPPINE WARS.

Prentis, Secs. 258-270; *Coll.*, VI: 130-147.

2. MATERIAL ADVANCE.
    a. Development of Agriculture.
    b. Railroads.
    c. Mining.
    d. Manufacture.

Prentis, Secs. 366-7, 393, 403, and all of Ch. XXXIV; Spring, Ch. 14; *Coll.*, VIII: 143-8; XI: 80-215 (especially good); XII: 37-64; Reports of Secretary of State Board of Agriculture; Census Reports; U. S. Statistical Abstracts.

3. GROWTH AND DISTRIBUTION OF POPULATION.

Prentis, passim; Census Bulletins; U. S. Statistical Abstracts.

4. POLITICAL AND SOCIAL PROGRESS. Tendencies. Place in the Eyes of the Nation Compared with Territorial Period.
    a. Parties and Elections, 1898-1912. State and National.
    b. Legislative Advance.
    c. Constitutional Advance. Supreme Court. Equal Suffrage.
    d. Attitude of Kansas on National Questions.

Prentis, Chs. XXX-XXXIV, passim; *Coll.*, XII: 69-77, 359-75,

396-401; Journals of House and Senate of Kansas; Statutes ("Session Laws") of Kansas, 1898-1913; Periodical Literature and Newspapers; Reports of Board of Control, Attorney-General, State Bank Commissioner, and other State Boards and Commissions; General Statutes of Kansas, 1909.

IX. Schools and Churches. 1854-1913.

1. SCHOOLS. The Policy.
    a. Common Schools.
    b. Secondary Schools.
    c. Institutions for Higher Learning. Public and Private.

Prentis, Secs. 117, 132, 133, 178, 238, 239, 278, and Ch. XXXV; Spring, passim; *Annals*, passim; Andreas, passim; *Coll.*, VI: 70-75, 114-21; VII: 167-88, 502-20; XI: 424-55; XII: 69, 77-98, 195-217; Kansas Constitution, clauses concerning education; Walters, *History of Agricultural College;* "Session Laws" to date.

2. THE CHURCH IN KANSAS.
    a. Church Beginnings.
    b. Home Missionaries and Church Extension.
    c. Present Status of Denominations.

Prentis, Spring, *Annals*, and Andreas, passim. *Coll.*, VII: 494-500; VIII: 250-7; XI: 19-46, 489-528; XII; 77-98, 135-82. Various denominational reports, and publications.

X. Men, Women, and Letters in Kansas.

1. NOTED MEN AND WOMEN OF KANSAS.
    a. Statesmen and Soldiers.
    b. Writers.
    c. Scientists.
    d. Educators.

Prentis, Secs. 310-19 (esp.), and scattering references throughout; Spring, passim; *Cyclopedia of Kansas History*, Vol. III, and indexes of all volumes of Historical Collections for biographical sketches, addresses, etc. Biographies cited above. Periodical Literature.

2. KANSAS IN LITERATURE.
    a. History and Biography.
    b. Essay.
    c. Fiction.
    d. Poetry.
    e. Journalism.

Prentis, Ch. XXXVI; Carruth, *Kansas in Literature;* Kansas Magazine (old); Kansas Magazine (now); Books by Kansas Authors; Periodical Literature; Newspapers of Kansas.

BIBLIOGRAPHY.

American Historical Reports. Vol. I. (1906). Washington. 1906.
American Historical Review. Vols. IV and VI. New York.
Ames, Herman V. State Documents on Federal Relations. Philadelphia. 1906.
Andreas, A. T. History of the State of Kansas. Chicago. 1883.
Appleton. Cyclopedia of American Biography. New York. 1900.
Babcock, K. C. The Rise of American Nationality. New York. 1906.
Bates, Frank G. Civics of Kansas. In Boynton's School Civics. Boston. 1910.
Becker, Carl. Kansas. In Turner Essays. New York. 1910.
Blackmar, F. W. Cyclopedia of Kansas History. Chicago. 1912.
Blackmar, F. W. Kansas. In Vol. IV of The Province and The States, ed. by W. A. Goodspeed. Madison. 1904.
Blackmar, F. W. Life of Charles Robinson. Topeka. 1902.
Boynton and Mason. Journey Through Kansas. Cincinnati. 1855.
Brewerton, G. Douglas. War in Kansas. New York. 1856.
Brower, G. W. Quivira Society Publications.
Brown, G. W. Rescue of Kansas. Rockford. 1902.
Burgess, John W. The Middle Period. New York. 1905.
Butler, Rev. Pardee. Recollections. Cincinnati. 1889.
Carruth, W. H. Kansas in Literature. Topeka. 1900.
Case, Nelson. History of Labette County. Topeka. 1893.
Connelly, W. E. Life of John Brown. Topeka. 1900.
Connelly, W. E. Lives of Territorial Governors.
Cordley, Richard. History of Lawrence. Lawrence. 1895.
Cordley, Richard. Pioneering in Kansas. Boston. 1903.
Crawford, Samuel J. Kansas in the Sixties. Chicago. 1911.
Gihon, John H. Geary in Kansas. Philadelphia. 1857.
Goodlander, C. W. Early Days of Fort Scott. Fort Scott. 1900.
Hale, Edward E. Kanzas and Nebraska. Boston. 1854.
Hart, Albert Bushnell. American History told by Contemporaries. Vol. IV. New York. 1906.
Hodder, Frank H. Government of the People of Kansas. Bound with Thorpe's Civil Government. New York. 1901.

Hodder, Frank H. Some Aspects of the English Bill. Vol. X of "Coll." and Vol. I, Am. Hist. Reports for 1906.
Holloway, J. N. History of Kansas. Lafayette, Ind. 1868.
Ingalls, John J. Writings. Kansas City. 1902.
Inman, Henry. The Great Salt Lake Trail. Topeka. 1899.
Jenkins, Jeff. The Northern Tier. Topeka. 1880.
Kansas, General Statutes of. 1909. Topeka. 1909.
Kansas, Laws of. "Session Laws" for all Sessions. Topeka.
Kansas Magazine (old). Topeka.
Kansas Magazine (new). Wichita.
Kansas State Historical Society. Collections. Vols. I-XII. Topeka.
Kansas Territory, Statutes of ("Bogus Statutes"). 1855.
Kellogg, Florence. Mother Bickerdyke. Chicago. 1907.
Lalor, John J. Cyclopedia of Political Science, etc. Chicago. 1883.
Larned, J. N. History for Ready Reference. Springfield. 1895.
Macdonald, William. Documentary Source Book of American History. New York. 1908.
Macdonald, William. Select Documents. New York. 1905.
Martin, Geo. W. Boundary Lines of Kansas. In "Collections" and in Vol. III Miss. Valley Hist. Asso. Proceedings.
Martin, Geo. W. Fifty Years of Kansas. Topeka.
Martin, John A. Addresses. Topeka. 1888.
Mississippi Valley Historical Association, Proceedings of. Vol. III.
Newton, John. Capt. John Brown. New York. 1902.
Parkman, Francis. La Salle and the Discovery of the Great West. Boston. 1907.
Perkins, Margaret. Echoes of Pawnee Rock. Wichita. 1908.
Pike, Zebulon M. Account of Expedition. 1808.
Prentis, Noble. History of Kansas. Topeka. 1909.
Ray, P. O. Repeal of the Missouri Compromise. Cleveland. 1909.
Realf, Richard. Free State Poems. Topeka.
Rebellion Record. Washington.
Redpath, James. Life of John Brown. Boston. 1910.
Rhodes, James Ford. History of the United States. Vols. I and II. New York. 1896.
Robinson, Charles. The Kansas Conflict. New York. 1892.
Robinson, Sarah T. L. Kansas: Its Interior and Exterior Life. Boston. 1856.
Sanborn, F. B. Life and Letters of John Brown. Boston. 1885.

Sanborn, F. B. Recollections of Seventy Years. Manchester, N. H. 1908.
Savage, I. O. History of Republic County. Topeka. 1883.
Schouler, James. History of the United States. Vol. V. New York. 1894.
Six Months in Kansas, by a lady (H. A. R.). Boston. 1856.
Speer, John. Life of James H. Lane. Garden City, Kan. 1896
Spring, L. W. Kansas. New York. 1906.
Stark, Andrew. Kansas Annual Register for 1864. Leavenworth. 1864.
Thayer, Eli. The Kansas Crusade. New York. 1899.
Thompson, Matt. Early History of Wabaunsee County. Alma, Kan. 1901.
Three Years on the Kansas Border. By a Clergyman of the Episcopal Church. New York. 1856.
Tomlinson, W. P. Kansas in 1858. New York. 1859.
Treaties and Conventions. Washington. 1889.
Turner, Frederick Jackson. Rise of the New West. New York. 1906.
Villard, O. G. Life of John Brown. Boston. 1910.
Von Holst, H. Constitutional History of the United States, 1850-'54. Chicago. 1885.
Von Holst, H. Life of John Brown. Boston. 1888.
Walters, J. D. History of Kansas Agricultural College. Manhattan. 1909.
Ware, Eugene. Poems of Ironquill. Chicago. 1892.
Wilder, D. W. Annals of Kansas. Topeka. 1886.
Winship, G. P. Coronado. Reports of American Bureau of Ethnology. Vol. XIV.
Winship, G. P. Journey of Coronado. Trailmaker Series. New York. 1904.
Winsor, Justin. Narrative and Critical History of America. Vols. I, II, and IV. Boston. 1884-'86.

STANFORD UNIVERSITY LIBRARY

To avoid fine, this book should be returned on or before the date last stamped below.

CPSIA information can be obtained
at www.ICGtesting.com
Printed in the USA
BVHW041121190219
540638BV00018B/797/P